People of the Bible

The Bible through stories and pictures

The Birth of Jesus

First published in the United States of America 1982
by Raintree Publishers Limited Partnership
in association with Belitha Press Ltd., London.

Conceived, designed and produced by Belitha Press Ltd.,
2 Beresford Terrace, London N5 2DH

Library of Congress Cataloging in Publication Data

Storr, Catherine.
    The birth of Jesus.

        (People of the Bible)
        Summary: A simple retelling of the birth of Jesus;
the visits by the shepherds and wise men; and the return
of Mary, Joseph, and Jesus to Nazareth to live.
        1. Jesus Christ—Nativity—Juvenile literature.
[I. Jesus Christ—Nativity. 2. Bible stories—N.T.]
I. Rowe, Gavin, ill. II. Title. III. Series.
BT315.2.S76   1982   226′.09505   82-9048

Published by the Children's Reading Institute
Durham, Connecticut 06422 USA
Scarborough, Ontario M1R 3C5 Canada

The Birth of
Jesus

RETOLD BY CATHERINE STORR
PICTURES BY GAVIN ROWE

Children's Reading Institute

Durham, CT
Scarborough, ONT

Belitha Press Limited • London

For a long time, the Jews had been ruled by King Herod, who was cruel and wicked.

One day, an angel appeared to Mary, a Jewish girl, and said, "Mary! You are going to have a baby son, who will become King of all the Jews."

Mary was astonished. She said, "But I'm not even married."

The angel replied, "Don't worry. This will be God's child, Jesus."

The angel also visited a carpenter called Joseph, who wanted to marry Mary. The angel said, "Mary is going to have a very special baby. He will be a great King and the child of God."

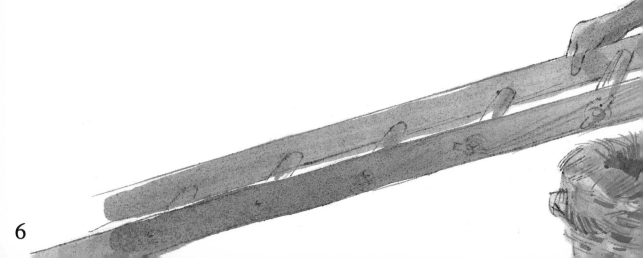

7

Joseph and Mary were married and lived in Nazareth. Just before the baby was ready to be born they had to go to Bethlehem.

As they were arriving in Bethlehem Mary said to Joseph, "We must find somewhere to stay—the baby is going to be born very soon."

Joseph went from door to door, asking, "Can we stay here?"

But every house was full. Even the inn had no rooms to spare. But the innkeeper was sorry for Mary. He said, "You can rest in the stable with the animals, if you like."

That night, Mary's baby was born in the stable. Mary put him to bed on the straw in the manger. She told Joseph, "We'll call him Jesus."

All around were the animals—cows, donkeys, camels, sheep, a goat. They all looked at the tiny, sleepy baby.

That same night, some shepherds were in a nearby field, looking after their sheep. Suddenly they saw a bright light and an angel. They were frightened.

15

16

But the angel said, "Don't be afraid. I
bring good news. The King you've been
waiting for is here at last. He is a tiny baby,
lying in a manger in a stable in Bethlehem."

Then the shepherds saw many more
angels. They were singing, "Glory to God in
the highest."

The shepherds hurried off to Bethlehem and found the stable. They went in and saw Mary and Joseph with Jesus, and the beasts standing around. They were very excited, and went away to tell everyone what had happened.

Far away in the East, some wise men saw a new and brilliant star. They guessed that at last the King of the Jews had been born. They made the long journey to Jerusalem. When they got there they went to King Herod, and told him they had come to look for the new King.

When King Herod heard there was another King, he was troubled. He said to the wise men, "Go and find this child, and then come back and tell me about him." Actually he planned to kill the baby King.

The wise men set off again after the bright star. It led them to Bethlehem. It seemed to be just over the roof of the stable where Mary and Joseph and Jesus were.

The wise men went into the stable and
saw Jesus. They gave him rich gifts—gold,
frankincense, and myrrh.

That night God told the wise men in a dream not to tell King Herod about the baby. So they went back to their homes in the far East.

When the wise men did not come back to Jerusalem, Herod knew he had been tricked. He ordered his soldiers to kill all the baby boys in Bethlehem.

29

An angel told Joseph, "Take Mary and the baby and go to Egypt. There you will be safe from wicked King Herod."

So Joseph and Mary set off in the dark, and escaped from Herod's soldiers. They stayed in Egypt until Herod was dead.

Then it was safe for them to come back to their home in Nazareth, where Joseph worked as a carpenter.

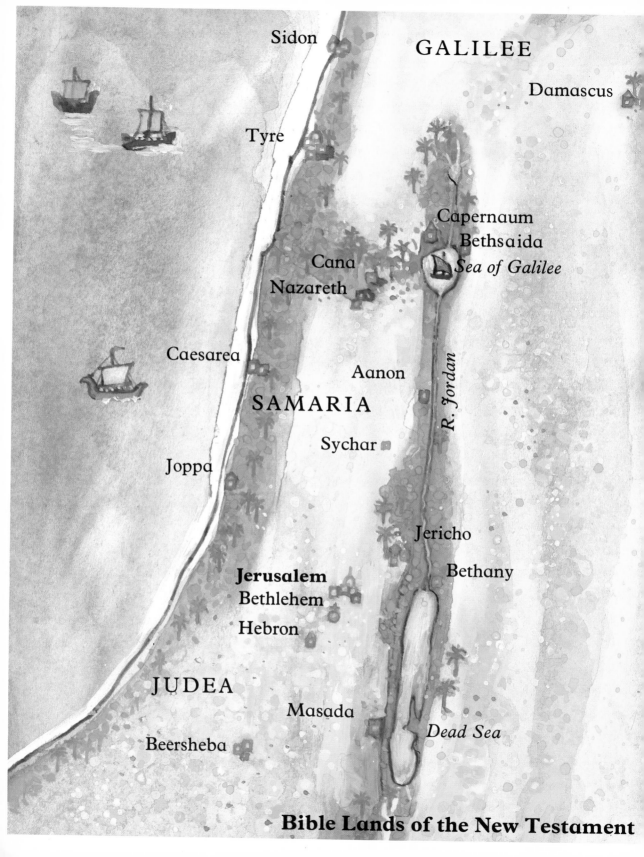

Sidon

GALILEE

Damascus

Tyre

Capernaum
Bethsaida
Sea of Galilee

Cana
Nazareth

Caesarea

Aanon

SAMARIA

Sychar

Joppa

R. Jordan

Jericho

Bethany

Jerusalem
Bethlehem

Hebron

JUDEA

Masada

Dead Sea

Beersheba

Bible Lands of the New Testament